champagne &
sparkling wines

champagne & sparkling wines

a complete guide to
sparkling wines of the world

susie barrie

MITCHELL BEAZLEY

champagne & sparkling wines

by Susie Barrie

First published in Great Britain in 2004
by Mitchell Beazley, an imprint of Octopus
Publishing Group Limited, 2–4 Heron Quays,
London E14 4JP.

A CIP catalogue record for this book is
available from the British Library.

ISBN: 1 84000 845 8

The author and publishers will be grateful
for any information which will assist them
in keeping future editions up to date.
Although all reasonable care has been taken
in the preparation of this book, neither
the publishers nor the author can accept
any liability for any consequences arising
from the use thereof, or the information
contained therein.

Commissioning editor   Hilary Lumsden
Executive art editor   Yasia Williams
Photographer   Tory McTernan
Managing editors   Emma Rice, Julie Sheppard
Design   Tim Pattinson
Editor   Diona Gregory
Production   Gary Hayes
Index   Laura Hicks

Mitchell Beazley would like to thank the following
companies and Champagne houses for their
assistance with the photography: Billecart-Salmon,
Laurent-Perrier, Gosset, Pol Roger, Jacquesson,
Pommery, Veuve Clicquot, Waterloo Wine Company.

Typeset in RotisSansSerif

Printed and bound by
Toppan Printing Company in China

contents

introduction

There are certain things in life that only ever bring happiness and, for me, sparkling wine would be very close to the top of my top ten. Because it is such a celebratory drink, we're sometimes guilty of grouping all sparkling wines together and forgetting that a huge variety of styles exist, all of which can be appropriate for different occasions. The best Champagnes are quite simply some of the most heavenly liquids you'll ever drink, but in many situations another wine will be perfectly adequate if not, at times, more suitable.

Through the pages of this little book I aim to introduce you to fizz you might never have encountered before, to explain some of the styles you're used to drinking but have never really understood, and to steer you in the right direction when choosing the best bottle for the occasion. Although I've tasted sparkling wines from places as far afield as Lithuania and Transylvania, I hope you'll forgive me for sticking here to the more obvious options. If you've even picked up this book I know you must be of a like mind, so indulge me now and relax as we enter the glorious, fizz-induced haze of the world of sparkling wine.

It's important to understand how sparkling wines are made, not to bore your dinner guests with talk of second fermentations, but so that you can appreciate why some sparklers taste so much better than others – and cost a little more, too.

unravelling the mystery

The traditional method

The traditional method of making sparkling wine, the *méthode traditionnelle*, used to make all Champagne and other quality sparkling wines around the world, involves two fermentations, with the second, the bubble creator, taking place in the bottle from which you'll eventually fill your glass.

Put simply, when making Champagne or traditional method sparkling wine, the winemaker first makes an ordinary still wine called the base wine or *vin clair*, ideally a dry and fairly acidic wine. This is then blended with other base wines to create the desired style (all Champagne houses have their own particular house style that they aim to recreate year on year). A mixture of sugar and yeast is then added, the *liqueur de tirage*, that causes a second fermentation to occur in the bottle creating the all-important bubbles.

The wine, which is now sparkling, will be left for several months, and in some cases years, to allow the dead yeast cells remaining in the bottle to impart their rich flavours. Finally the yeast is removed or "disgorged", traditionally by the labour-intensive method of riddling by hand, but now more usually using a large computerized metal cage known as a gyropalette. The bottle is topped up with a mixture of wine and sugar syrup, the *dosage*, and finally the cork is put in place. The label will state that the wine is "*méthode traditionnelle*".

What you should be looking for in a top-quality Champagne or sparkling wine are the finest bubbles, shooting to the top of your glass, accompanied by a whole host of delicious flavours.

The only way to achieve this is to implement the lengthy and labour-intensive process described above. That's why they're expensive, but heavenly experiences rarely come cheap.

The transfer method

This process begins in exactly the same way as the traditional method, but instead of riddling the wine to remove the yeast, the entire contents of the bottle, including the yeast, are emptied into a large tank, under pressure. The wine is filtered in bulk, the *dosage* is added and it's finally put into a fresh bottle.

Used mainly in the New World, this method produces wines with the flavour advantages of a second fermentation in bottle, but with less exciting bubbles. Its main plus point is that it's cheaper than the traditional method. The label will state "bottle-fermented" or "fermented in bottle" but not "fermented in *this* bottle".

The tank method

Developed by Eugene Charmat in the early twentieth century, this is also known as the Charmat method. The still base wine undergoes a second fermentation in a large tank: the cooler the temperature, the longer the fermentation, and the better the flavours.

When the wine is required for bottling, it's cooled, clarified, the *dosage* is added, and it's finally bottled – all under pressure. This method is cheap and fast, and best suited to aromatic grape varieties that are not intended for long ageing.

The wines are usually light and easy-drinking without any of the complexities gained from fermentation in bottle. Most of the vast quantities of sekt produced in Germany are made in this way, and the Italian Asti DOCG (*Denominazione di Origine Controllata e Garantita*) has its own variation on this theme.

Carbonation or the "pompe à bicyclette"

Carbon dioxide is dissolved in a still wine before bottling takes place under pressure. Also known as the bicycle-pump method, the bubbles in the wine are created in much the same way as those in a fizzy soft drink. The wines have large bubbles which disappear fairly rapidly once poured – these wines may be cheap to make but that's exactly how they'll taste, so be warned!

We'll look at variations of the above four methods of producing sparkling wines as and when they appear in the following pages.

sparkling wines around the world

From France to New Zealand there are wonderful winemakers trying their hand at the intricate art of making wine sparkle. In New World countries such as Australia they tend to look to Champagne for both their methods and choice of grapes. But there are many Old World countries producing delicious wines that have their very own, unique charm. Let's take a look at what each country has to offer.

Almost 300 million bottles of Champagne are now produced each year, with the UK and the USA sitting in first and second position respectively as the biggest importers – but way behind the French who manage to knock back more than all their export markets put together, sensible chaps.

champagne

For as long as we can remember, Champagne has been *the* drink with which to celebrate an occasion, be it a wedding, a new baby, a new house, a birthday, an anniversary, passing an exam, or just getting to the end of a terrible week. So let's find the right Champagne, at the right price, for you.

Champagne styles – dry to sweet

Extra brut – Bone dry, having been topped up, post-disgorgement, with still wine to which no sugar syrup has been added.

Brut – Most of the decent non vintage (NV) Champagnes are brut, although levels of dryness tend to vary according to the house style.

Extra dry – Edging towards medium-dry.

Sec – As this style is best described as medium, its literal translation of "dry" is misleading, to say the least.

Demi-sec – Again confusing nomenclature as the wonderfully subtle sweetness of the best *demi-sec* Champagnes makes them ideal partners for light, fruit-based desserts.
Rich/doux – Rich and fabulously sweet.

The grapes

Chardonnay and the two black grapes, Pinot Noir and Pinot Meunier, are the only grape varieties permitted in the making of Champagne. Chardonnay, found mainly in the Côte des Blancs, gives a fine and lively, refreshing elegance to the wines in which it plays a part. The Pinot Noir of the Montagne de Reims offers backbone, structure, and longevity to the blend, while the fruity, early-ripening Pinot Meunier from the Vallée de la Marne provides flesh and balance.

Blanc de blancs – This is Champagne that is made solely from white Chardonnay grapes. Usually a finer and more tenacious style, with a certain femininity that sets it apart from the classic blend.

Blanc de noirs – As you'll probably have guessed, these Champagnes are exclusively the territory of the black varieties Pinot Noir and Pinot Meunier. They often have a slight pinky tinge due to their black skins, and are usually rich and full-bodied in style.

Big brands

Don't always look for a big brand name. If you're buying in quantity for a party, or you fancy a treat but don't want to fork out a fortune, then supermarket own-brands or small grower Champagnes are a superb choice. They're often half the price of the big boys who spend oodles of cash on marketing, and they can taste every bit as good, if not better.

Vintage vs non vintage (NV)

All Champagne houses produce a non vintage Champagne that expresses their own house style perfectly, and the idea is that it'll taste exactly the same whenever you buy it. In order to achieve this, the *chef de cave* will blend the base wines of the current vintage with several "reserve" wines from previous years, before the wines are bottled, prior to the second fermentation. The important thing is, of course, to know your house styles and to choose your own favourite which can, in theory, be purchased again and again without ever disappointing.

Recommended NV Champagnes

Louis Roederer Brut
Biscuity, apricot fruit, elegant, balanced, impeccable.

Veuve Clicquot Yellow Label
Fruity, brioche, robust.

Taittinger Brut Réserve
Light, pear fruit, floral, fresh.

Pol Roger Brut Réserve
Bright, crisp, lemon, white peach.

Vintage

In some years the harvest is so sublimely good that it's possible for the *chef de cave* to create a Champagne that perfectly expresses the house style without any need for the addition of reserve wines. In such years a "vintage" Champagne will be made and the label will carry the year of the vintage. These wines are a fascinating mix of house style with the complexities and unique characteristics of the given vintage. Good recent vintages are: 1982, 1985, 1988, 1989, 1990, 1995, 1996, and 1997.

The issue of ageing

A non vintage Champagne, once it hits the shops' shelves, is intended for immediate drinking, although an extra six months or a year in bottle can often add another dimension of rounded complexity to the wine, especially if on initial tasting it seems a little too crisp and austere. Leave the top NVs for a few years and I doubt you'll be disappointed by the result. Vintage Champagnes are usually not released until at least seven years after the vintage, and the best (*see* page 18) will continue to develop and improve for many years to come.

Prestige cuvée

Most Champagne houses now produce one wine that crowns their range and offers the ultimate in terms of luxury, quality, and indeed price. The wine will only be produced using grapes from the best years, from the best vineyards – usually *grand cru* – and with all the care and attention that it's possible to lavish on a single wine. Usually vintage dated, they are *very* expensive, but they are also some of the most exquisite wines you're ever likely to drink.

Here's a small selection of what's available today:
Louis Roederer Cristal – Tsar Alexander II asked for a Champagne to be made and put into a clear glass crystal bottle for him in 1877, hence the name.
Moët & Chandon Dom Pérignon – named after the man who mythology would have us believe was responsible for inventing Champagne.
Pol Roger Cuvée Winston Churchill – Sir Winston Churchill wrote that, "Champagne should be a daily

Recommended NV Champagnes cont.

Fleury Père et Fils Brut
Biodynamic. Floral, perfumed, lightly tropical, smoky.

Jacquesson Cuvée No 728
Full-bodied, praline, nuts, power.

Henriot Brut Souverain
Bready, savoury, elegant, pear/apple fruit.

Bollinger Special Cuvée
Big, nutty, woody, masculine.

Billecart-Salmon Brut Réserve
Spice, red apple, rich, bready.

Krug Grande Cuvée
Full, rich, toasty, spicy fruit, stylish. This elegant wine could be classed as a prestige cuvée, because only top-quality grapes and older than usual reserve wines are used, hence the hefty price tag.

delight for those who know the true meaning of life," and who would argue with Churchill?

Pommery Cuvée Louise – the 1989 is tasting stunning as I write.

Taittinger Comtes de Champagne Blanc de Blancs – for those who love the elegance of Chardonnay Champagne.

Rosé Champagne

Glamorous, sexy, hedonistic – whether it's a picnic in the park, the wedding morning with the girls, or the most romantic meal of your life, rosé will never fail to delight. Rosé Champagnes are made in one of two ways: either by blending in a little still red wine from the region before bottling, or by allowing the skins of the black grapes to stay in contact with the juice just long enough for some of the colour to seep into the wine.

With its soft, red-fruit flavours and rich, full body, rosé is one of the best Champagnes to match with food – especially sushi.

Most of the classic regions of France produce their own version of a *crémant*. The term was originally used to describe less fizzy Champagnes, but when in the late 1980s the EU stopped "*méthode champenoise*" being used on the labels of wines made outside the Champagne region, *crémant* was adopted to describe traditional method sparkling wines produced throughout France.

other french
sparkling wines

Made in the same way as Champagne, and with quality a top priority, these *crémant* wines are a good bet if you're looking for a decent French alternative to the real thing. The grape varieties and terroirs vary from region to region, but all have strict controls on production. The main regions are Alsace, Die, Bourgogne (Burgundy), Loire, Limoux, Bordeaux, and Jura. Most decent NVs will taste better if you leave them alone for a couple of years. The vintage *cuvées* need a minimum of three years, with the best improving for up to seven or eight.

Alsace
Crémant d'Alsace – one of the best *crémants* you'll find, from the northeast of the country where France borders Germany. The appellation was created in 1976. Made from

a blend that usually includes a large proportion of Pinot Blanc, along with Pinot Gris, Pinot Noir, Auxerrois, Riesling, and increasingly Chardonnay, this is an elegant fizz with finely tuned bubbles and refreshingly crisp acidity. Production has increased fifteen-fold since the appellation was created and quality is consistently on the up.

The Loire Valley

Sparkling Saumur, Vouvray, Touraine, Montlouis, and Crémant de Loire – these are just the fizzy finds that you'll encounter along the banks of France's Loire River. Permitted varieties include Chenin Blanc, Cabernet Franc, Chardonnay, Sauvignon Blanc, Gamay, and Pinot Noir. No wonder French wine can get a little confusing at times.

Most of the sparkling wines produced in this region, aptly nicknamed "the garden of France", come from the central section of Anjou, Saumur, and Touraine. In many ways Saumur is the home of the region's sparkling wine industry, as it was here, in the early nineteenth century that Saumur sparkling wines were first created by Jean Ackerman, a Belgian who'd trained in Champagne. The maze of caves which have been carved out from the chalky tufa cliffs over the years, when building materials for the grand châteaux were required, provide maturation facilities that mirror very closely those of Champagne.

Saumur – made by the traditional method from fruit grown in chalky soils similar to those found in the Champagne region around Reims and Epernay, the only

Is Champagne always the best choice?

There are good Champagnes and bad, just as there are some wonderful and some utterly dire sparkling wines being made worldwide. The big brand names of Champagne are usually pretty consistent – they have to be, their livelihoods depend on it. But that consistency comes at a price. Equally, you'll find some great small grower Champagnes, particularly under supermarket own-labels (see page 15). Your safest route to quality and value for money is to head for the New World, where traditional method wines can be as good as, if not better than, many Champagnes and they are usually half the price. The warmer climate means that these wines tend to be fruitier and fuller in style, very appealing to those who don't like anything too sharp, or to those drinking fizz all night.

Safe popping

When opening any sparkling wine make sure that the bottle is well chilled. Hold it with the neck pointing away from you at a forty-five degree angle and, with one hand held firmly over and around the cork to counter the pressure of the bubbles, twist the base of the bottle with the other hand in an anti-clockwise direction until the cork removes itself with a gentle "phfutt".

real difference lies in the grapes. Almost all the Loire varieties are permitted, although, in practice, the dominant grape is Chenin Blanc, arguably the Loire's most famous. These wines are usually light and fresh with appley fruit flavours, but seldom have the complexity or elegance of Champagne.

Crémant de Loire – here grapes from Touraine and Anjou can also be used, giving the winemaker a little more freedom when blending. The percentage of the classic Champagne grapes tends to be higher, the yields have to be lower and the ageing time in bottle a little longer. All of which adds up to a better chance of decent fizz in your glass. With Saumur you have tradition, with Crémant present-day innovation. Both are made in the image of Champagne, offer value for money, and are certainly worth trying.

Vouvray – anyone who can even begin to guess what might be in their bottle labelled "Vouvray" deserves a medal. From dry and fruity to lusciously sweet, and from flat to frothy, it's a minefield. The cork and wire should give the game away as far as fizz is concerned (this is some of the Loire's best).

A few other quirky styles

St-Péray – from a small commune in the Rhône Valley, this traditional method, rustic, deep-coloured fizz is made from Marsanne and Roussanne grapes. Tiny amounts are now produced so, if you do find a bottle, give it a go.

Crémant de Die and Clairette de Die – rather confusingly Crémant de Die is a dry, traditional method sparkling wine made from the Clairette grape, while Clairette de Die is made from grapey Muscat Blanc. It's a light, floral, refreshingly sweetish sparkler and one of the first French wines ever made. The method used, the *méthode dioise*, relies on the inherent grape sugar to produce the second fermentation in bottle. The resulting wine is gently aromatic with all the flavours of the Muscat grape perfectly preserved.

Blanquette de Limoux and Crémant de Limoux – at the Abbey of St Hilaire, Limoux, in the southern France's Languedoc, it's believed that the Benedictine monks were making sparkling wine by the *méthode rurale* as far back as 1531, long before Champagne got in on the act. The grapes used are Mauzac (locally known as Blanquette), Chenin Blanc, and Chardonnay, with Mauzac playing a smaller role in the modern *crémant* style.

Champagne by any other name

Various Champagne houses, keen to jump on the New World bandwagon, have set up camp in Australia, New Zealand, California or Argentina. Look out for the house name on the label and you'll get the best of both worlds – tradition and experience *and* sunshine and innovation.

When we think of sparkling wine and Spain, the first word that immediately springs to mind is cava, and so it should, considering that it accounts for ninety to ninety-five per cent of Spain's total sparkling wine production.

spain – cava & others

A traditional method sparkling wine, cava was first made (on a commercial scale) in 1872 by Don José Raventós in the family cellars of Codorníu, in the town of Sant Sadurní d'Anoia, barely a stone's throw away from the beautiful city of Barcelona.

In fact, ninety-five per cent of all cava comes from this northeast province of Catalonia, and around three-quarters of the production centres around the town of Sant Sadurní.

The word *cava* means underground cellar in Spanish and from 1970 it was adopted as the generic name for sparkling wines made by the traditional method. This move came in response to the French seeking to stop the use of terms such as *champaña* and *método champañé* being used for wines made outside the Champagne region.

Although it took some time for the name to be fully embraced, by the time Spain joined the EU in 1986, the term cava was a well-known name and was recognized worldwide.

The grapes

Cava may be made by the traditional method but that doesn't mean that the Champagne threesome – Chardonnay, Pinot Noir, and Pinot Meunier – are going to be at their happiest in this particular part of the world or produce the most suitable fruit for top-quality cava. The grapes must come from listed vineyards and the traditional trio used in white cava are local varieties, little known outside Spain, and certainly not names we'd easily recognize.

Xarel-lo adds weight to the wine. The Parellada grape gives a light, creamy elegance to the blend. It's also used to make some lovely still wines, such as Miguel Torres' deliciously quaffable Viña Sol. Macabeo (Viura) – one of the main grapes used in white Rioja – lifts the wine with its characteristic freshness and acidity. Subirat (Malvasía Riojana) can also be blended in, as can Chardonnay, which was officially authorized for use in cava in 1986, and is proving increasingly popular with many winemakers.

A question of timing

The minimum ageing for cava is nine months. If you see *reserva* on the label then that ageing period jumps to three years and *gran reserva* wines require five years of ageing on the lees. One of the differences between a regular NV cava and Champagne is that the cava will be ready for drinking at just a year old, while Champagne has a longer minimum ageing period (*see* pages 16–17).

Raventós i Blanc

Founded in 1986 by part of the same family that created the first cava in 1872, this house is based in Sant Sadurní d'Anoia. It cannot be recommended highly enough, not only for its great cavas, but also because it knows about smart packaging – something sorely lacking at many a cava house. The "L'Hereu Brut" is a joy and a wonderful example of just what can be achieved from these oddball grapes when they're treated with a little understanding.

Cordoníu

A producer that was at the forefront of experimentation with Champagne varieties, it makes a wide range of cavas that includes a *rosado* from Pinot Noir. The "Anna de Cordoníu" *blanco*, a blend of seventy per cent Chardonnay with Parellada and Macabeo, is the biggest selling sparkling wine in Spain.

Albet i Noya

Founded at the end of the 1970s by Josep Maria Albet i Noya, this is a young company that produces fresh and appealing organic wines on the family estate.

A question of sweetness

Most cavas available to buy will be extra brut (bone-dry) or brut (dry), which is how most of us like our fizz. However, just as with Champagne, levels of sweetness rise up, through extra *seco*, *seco* and *semi-seco* to the ultimate indulgence of *dulce* (containing over fifty grams/litre of residual sugar) to accompany those heavenly *crema catalanyas* that this area specializes in.

Rosado/rosé

A handy option if you're looking for inexpensive pink fizz, Spanish rosé is made from Monastrell and/or Garnacha. Sometimes the Trepat and Pinot Noir grapes are also used.

The producers

The two biggest players, by quite some way, are Cordoníu and Freixenet, who, as well as providing a considerable chunk of what's consumed in Spain, share around ninety per cent of the export market.

Cordoníu is worth a visit as its buildings were designed by a contemporary of the architect Gaudí, and the site is now a national monument.

But there are also a couple of great, lesser-known producers that you'll hopefully come across in your local supermarket or tapas bar.

Breakfast bucks

Although cava is made by the traditional method and is, at best, a super glass of fizz, it'll never hit the heights in the way a good Champagne can. So when you're planning your next brunch party don't waste decent Champagne on the all-essential buck's fizz. Instead, mix equal quantities of cava with freshly squeezed orange juice for a wonderful breakfast beverage – I promise you won't be able to taste the difference. This way you'll have more left in the budget, too, for really good, properly smoked salmon to go with freshly scrambled eggs and hot buttered muffins.

Italy is the home of one of the best and most diverse ranges of food and wine in the world. It's also responsible for the most delightful apéritif imaginable, Prosecco.

italy – prosecco & others

Prosecco

This is the name of both the grape and the sparkling wine it's used to make, in the cool, hilly region just north of Venice. This stunningly beautiful area has frighteningly steep vineyards that demand the back-breaking tasks of being worked and picked by hand. It is all the more surprising then that, even at the top level, this is not an expensive drink.

What's in the bottle? The fact that both Champagne and Prosecco are sparkling is about the only thing that they have in common. Prosecco is a fresh, light, and intensely aromatic wine with primary fruit and floral flavours (apricots, apples, and jasmine), and relatively low levels of alcohol.

What you need to know and look out for – Prosecco should always be from the most recent vintage, which means that there's no need for a date to appear on the label, and it should be drunk within six months of being bottled.

DOC (*Denominazione di Origine Controllata*) is the demarcated area that encompasses the best vineyard slopes. Avoid Prosecco from the undemarcated plains.

In terms of sweetness it can be brut, the driest form of Prosecco, or extra dry, which is a little sweeter. The brut is a less traditional style, developed to suit international tastes, but I think the extra dry is a far better drink with the added touch of sweetness lending a soft roundness essential to the enjoyment of this light, easy-drinking fizz.

Valdobbiadene and Conegliano are the places where you'll find the best Prosecco being produced, so look out for these names on the label.

Franciacorta

It's only in the last few decades that Franciacorta has emerged as a region capable of producing top-quality sparkling wines, and the fact that they're made in the image of Champagne really sets them apart from Italy's other sparkling wines.

Situated in Lombardy, in the centre of north Italy, Franciacorta is home to some of the finest, and most expensive, sparkling wines this country has to offer. It gained DOCG status in 1995 and the rules of production are rigorously controlled by the local consortium CVF.

The wine must spend at least eighteen months (thirty months if it's a vintage wine) on its lees after the *prise de mousse*. Chardonnay tends to dominate most blends,

Top Prosecco producers

Adami

Bisol

Ruggeri

de Faveri

Nino Franco

Foss Marai

Carpenè Malvolti

Top Franciacorta producers

Ca' del Bosco

Bellavista

Cavalleri

with the other permitted varieties being Pinot Nero (France's Pinot Noir) and Pinot Bianco (Pinot Blanc).

Sweet or dry? These wines can be totally dry and will then be labelled *pas dosé*, *dosage zero* or *nature*. There's just a touch of sweetness in the extra brut, which rises steadily through brut, extra dry and *sec*, to *semi-sec*, where you'll find a delicious partner for your post-pasta panna cotta or tiramisu.

One to try – "Bellavista Franciacorta Cuvée Brut NV" is a blend of eighty-five per cent Chardonnay and fifteen per cent of the Pinots Bianco and Nero, this is a wonderfully elegant glass of fizz. Richly savoury with a creamy coating, smoky wild dried herbs mingle with ripe peach fruit and a vibrant mouthful of bubbles.

Other styles

Since gaining DOCG status in 1993, the quality of these two "Asti" wines has greatly improved.
Asti (Asti Spumante) – fizzier and more alcoholic than the superior Moscato d'Asti, this is a simple, sweetish sparkler that goes

wonderfully with a bowl of strawberries and cream in
the garden on a summer's afternoon. After the grapes
are pressed in the winery, the must is chilled and only
fermented when the wine is required for bottling. In this
way the intense fruit character and aroma of the Moscato
Bianco (Muscat) variety is preserved.

Moscato d'Asti – an aromatically grapey, delicately
fizzy, and lightly sweet dessert wine from Piedmont in
northeast Italy. Also made from the Moscato Bianco
grape, it shows much more character than Asti Spumante
as a result of it being made by small producers as
opposed to large companies. At a maximum of one
atmosphere of pressure in the bottle it's only just frothy
and, with a mere five to six per cent alcohol, it has a
wonderful lightness of touch.

Red sparklers from Piedmont

Freisa frizzante – in spite of its pale hue, the Freisa
grape produces a wine that is relatively high in tannin
and acidity. Combined with the unfermented sugar
that remains after a second fermentation in bottle,
it produces bitter-sweet flavours that may or may
not appeal.

Brachetto d'Acqui – made from the light red Brachetto
grape, this wine has the colour and flavour
of strawberries. Contero produces a deliciously floral
version weighing in at just five and a half per cent
alcohol – happy drinking.

For a nation that can at best be described as conservative, I never cease to be amazed by two little Teutonic anomalies I have come across on my travels. First, the Germanic (and indeed Austrian) eagerness to strip naked and let it all hang out in their beloved saunas and thermal baths, and secondly their inexhaustible thirst for (frankly frivolous) sparkling wine.

germany – sekt

Germans just can't get enough of it and each year they manage to knock back almost four litres per capita of fizz. A lot of this, however, comes in the form of very low-quality branded sekt (sparkling wine manufactured in Germany), from the big names such as Henkell Trocken. Most of these big companies were established around 1850 and produce volumes that run into millions of bottles per year.

The bulk of sekt is made from cheap base wines sourced outside Germany and then tank-fermented, to give what can only be described as very basic fizzy alcohol. Sadly, this is unlikely to change in spite of the fact that Germany's climate is potentially very well suited to the production of top-quality sparkling wines. The truth is that Germany is also the third largest importer of Champagne (over eleven million bottles in 2002), and it's only when this magic word appears on the label that the larger quanties of euros are readily expended.

Serving temperature

All sparkling wines and Champagnes should be served at 7–8°C (45–46°F). But for a rich vintage sparkler you may prefer it a little warmer to allow all the complex flavours to express themselves fully.

Sekt at its best

The quality wines – you may need to make your next holiday a trip up the Rhine if you're ever to taste these wines, as very few find their way out of the country. The stars of the sekt world are made from either Riesling grapes or one of the Pinots, and will no doubt have the words "Deutscher Sekt" on the label – a guarantee that only German base wine has been used. The name of the grape will usually appear too, along with a vintage date, in which case eighty-five per cent of the grapes will be from that variety and that particular vintage.

A sekt that states QbA on the label will have come from a specific wine-growing region, the name of which will also be on the label, ensuring 100 per cent of the grapes have come from that region. *Lagensekt* means that the wine is from a certain vineyard site, again detailed on the label, and in this case seventy-five per cent of the sekt will be from that specific vineyard site, while 100 per cent must still be from the region in question. As they're often estate-made in small quantities, they are usually bottle- rather than tank-fermented, and some are aged for up to ten years on the lees prior to release.

The words brut or extra-dry rather than the usual *trocken* (dry) or *halbtrocken* (medium-dry) will denote the level of dryness. Ernie Loosen, one of the Mosel region's very best and now most famous producers, makes a vintage Riesling brut, "1989 Bernkasteler Badstube Riesling Sekt", if you're looking for something special.

Sekt – the bare facts

In 1849 production totalled 1,270,000 bottles from approximately forty-three producers. Today, annual production is around five million bottles from approximately 1,000 producers.

Around ninety per cent of sekt made in Germany is based on cheap Italian, French and non-German still wines, mostly sold as dry (*trocken*) or medium-dry (*halbtroken*).

Ninety-eight per cent of all sekt is made by the tank method.

Most sekt tastes like alcoholic sparkling mineral water and should only be drunk while flying to Germany or Austria, when its quality will be on a par with the airline food.

Yes, believe it or not, the UK is capable of producing some excellent traditional method sparkling wines, and they're getting better all the time. It produces around 2.2 million bottles of wine a year and around a fifth of that is sparkling. In fact, the greatest potential for top-quality wine from England lies in its sparkling wines.

england

This is not surprising, really, when you consider how close England is to the north of France and the home of sparkling wine, Champagne. The relatively cool climate of the south of England is very similar to that of the Champagne region, and allows the same long, slow, ripening period necessary for the production of good base wines. The barrier that currently stands in the way of a full steam ahead approach to English sparkling wine has nothing to do with climate, soil or aspect, but rather a lack of confidence in what is, inevitably, a very expensive business. People are still feeling their way, experimenting

with different grape clones and gradually gaining the experience needed to succeed in a very competitive market-place. After all, the first sparkling wine to be produced commercially in England appeared just fifty or so years ago, so the industry is still very young.

As I write, around twenty-five producers in England are making sparkling wine, some exclusively, some as a part of their portfolio, with Nyetimber, based in West Sussex, sitting at the top of the tree in terms of international awards. If you're a fan of organics then Davenport, situated on the Kent/Sussex border, produces a delicious traditional method sparkling wine called "Limney". In a recent tasting the 1999 vintage was full of fresh, juicy flavours of lemons and apples. Other producers worthy of mention are Ridgeview and Chapel Down, whose range includes a very impressive rosé.

Many of the English wineries make a substantial part of their income from cellar-door sales and are therefore very keen to welcome visitors. So, if you're visiting the English countryside, why not head for an English vineyard? I think you'll be pleasantly surprised.

The spoon trick

Yes, it does work. If you find yourself in possession of a bottle of fizz that you haven't finished and want to save for the next day, simply dangle a teaspoon in the neck and pop it back in the refrigerator. It doesn't have to be silver, stainless steel will do just fine. The metal acts as a thermal conductor causing the air inside the bottle to cool (to below the temperature of the wine), and form an air cavity above the liquid, so stopping the bubbles from escaping. At least that's what I'm told and it hasn't failed me yet.

I don't know if you've noticed, but Californian wines are expensive, and rarely offer what could be deemed to be value for money when compared with their Chilean or southern French counterparts. But California is a glamorous, aspirational place, associated with wealth and abundance, and we seem to be prepared to pay over the odds for a little liquid sunshine that helps us to buy into that dream.

north america

In the 1970s and 1980s many of the big Champagne and cava houses took this fact and the domestic American market's love of sparkling wines to heart and invested heaps of cash in buying land and vineyards in the Golden State. It was important to find cool climate sites and two of the most promising areas proved to be Carneros, an area that straddles both Napa and Sonoma, and the more northwesterly Anderson Valley, close to the Pacific Ocean in Mendocino.

The good news for us is that the experience, and attention to detail, that the French (or Spanish) connection brings, means that these wines will rarely be of poor quality. They may not have all the complexity and elegance of the best Champagnes, but they're certainly more likely to please than disappoint. The bad news is that you'll pay about the same as you would for an average bottle of Champagne.

Schramsberg – Traditional method sparkling wine was first made in California as early as 1855. Experiments with both the Charmat and transfer methods were to follow before the classical method saw a revival (that continues today), when Jack and Jamie Davies bought Schramsberg (Calistoga) in 1965 and made California's first truly excellent traditional method sparkling wine from Champagne varieties. These are complex wines that will benefit from up to ten years ageing, and in a recent tasting the 1994 vintage (ninety per cent Pinot Noir), was deliciously developed and toasty with lots of rich, baked red-apple fruit along with a crisp, refreshing mousse.

Domaine Carneros – Established in 1987, this is Champagne Taittinger's California venture, which stays true to the Taittinger style in its fruity, light, and elegant way.

Roederer Estate – Unlike others who were convinced by Carneros' potential, Jean-Claude Rouzaud of Champagne Louis Roederer decided in 1982 that the Anderson Valley was the place to be. This cool, foggy region, located 201 kilometers (125 miles) north of San Francisco, proved a great choice, producing excellent fruit from Roederer's own vineyards for the Anderson Valley Brut (known as "Quartet" in Europe), a rosé and a top-of-the-range vintage dated wine, L'Ermitage.

Other top producers to look out for

Handley Cellars

Iron Horse Vineyards

Mumm Cuvée Napa
– *its offerings include a NV brut, a NV rosé and a NV blanc de blancs: all perfectly drinkable but hardly value for money.*

Bonny Doon
– *look out for two "Italian" variations. The 2000 Moscato del Solo Frizzante and the 2001 Freisa Frizzante.*

Wines from New York, Oregon and Washington State are all worth looking out for, too.

In the past few years Chilean and Argentinian wines have seen the kind of success that Australia enjoyed when its wines first hit our shelves over twenty years ago. We're talking about red and white still wines, though. I doubt if many people know that South America produces sparkling wine, let alone have tried it. It's a market that is still very much in its infancy, but if you do stumble across one of the exported brands then you're likely to find very quaffable fizz, at a very acceptable price.

south america

Who's doing it in Chile?

Two names you are likely to know are:

Valdivieso – familiar to most fans of Chilean wine, it's Chile's largest and oldest producer of sparkling wine. It makes 500,000 cases a year, a large chunk of which is consumed on home soil. Much of it is tank-fermented but there are some good traditional method wines and about a fifth of the total sparkling production is exported.

Miguel Torres – the extraordinary man responsible for revolutionizing Spanish wine also has a finger in the Chilean pie. Having already produced some lovely still wines, he's now turned his hand to sparkling wines and makes a good traditional method brut, a blend of thirty per cent Chardonnay and seventy per cent Pinot Noir that would liven up any celebration. The vineyard, which is situated south of Santiago in Chile's Curicó Valley, hasn't been exposed to a drop of insecticide, weedkiller or fungicide, so this is a good choice if you're prone to allergies.

Other names to look out for – good producers include Undurraga and Tarapacá.

And in Argentina?

Chandon Argentina – one of the most successful foreign ventures that the Champagne house Moët & Chandon has made. Pinot Noir, Chardonnay and Semillon, grown in the foothills of the Andes in Mendoza, make up the blend for this traditional method sparkler. Production is virtually organic and you're very likely to see this one in your local store at half the price of an average bottle of Champagne.

Toso – a name that's recently hit the shelves with a basic Charmat method brut and a superior traditional method extra-brut. Pascual Toso of Mendoza is the second largest producer of fizz in Argentina and a blend of Chardonnay and Chenin Blanc is used to create these easygoing wines.

Cepas de Mendoza – a new venture, begun in 2001, with the intention of producing quality sparkling wines at everyday prices. The classic varieties of Chardonnay and Pinot Noir are used to create three different blends for supermarkets, independents, and restaurants. If you're dining out then "Gala" will be the name on the label.

Flat and round or tall and slender?

Drinking from a glass that was allegedly modelled on Marie Antoinette's breasts might seem appealing, but it's a hopeless shape for fizz – far too much surface area from which the bubbles can escape. Always choose a tall, slim, flute-shaped glass, and you'll be sure to enjoy fresh and lively bubbles from beginning to end.

From upfront, cheap, and cheerful quaffers, packed with big bubbles and easygoing fruity flavours, to the elegance of top-quality traditional method wines made from cool-climate fruit, this part of the southern hemisphere has something for everyone. Even red wine drinkers can look forward to fizz in this, the home of rich and spicy sparkling Shiraz.

australia & new zealand

Australia

One of the main reasons that Australian wines have been so hugely successful over the last couple of decades is their makers' ability to offer us what we want (even if we don't know what that is until we're faced with it), when we want it, and at a price we're happy to pay – and sparkling wine is no exception.

Lots of big companies whose wines you'll already know and recognize, and feel safe with, are now producing sparklers under the same brand names. A bit like their partner still wines, they're unlikely to offer subtlety or complexity, but they'll be fizzy, fruity, and eminently acceptable as a party wine.

Sparkling Shiraz is bold, fresh, spicy, and packed with juicy, peppery, black cherry fruit. At its most basic level it's great fun to serve at a barbecue, being a better partner for smoky, meaty flavours than a basic white fizz would be. If, however, you're looking for something extra special, and are prepared to pay the price, then Charles Melton in the Barossa Valley can offer a "Sparkling Red" (Shiraz and Cabernet Sauvignon) that'll blow you away.

The Champagne connection

As is nearly always the case, the best sparkling wines Australia has to offer come from the cooler climate pockets of production and are made in the image of Champagne.

"Cool" in Australian terms is only in comparison to the rest of the country and, more often than not, the elegance of the wines will be matched by bolder, more forward fruit flavours than those found in most Champagnes. This can be great if you fancy fizz and you're going to be eating Asian or Pacific Rim foods, or if you find most mid-range Champagnes just too dry and acidic for your taste.

The Champagne house Moët & Chandon saw the potential here and established Domaine Chandon Australia in Victoria's Yarra Valley in 1985. The wines have been sold under the "Green Point" label in the UK, and the range includes vintage and NV wines, rosé, and a stunning blanc de blancs.

As well as those establishments with a Champagne connection, there are people making wonderful wines, capable of rivalling many a good Champagne, and using the same method, but without a drop of French blood. Too many exist to mention them all, but just look out for "traditional method" on the label, spend as much as you would on a basic Champagne and see what you can find.

New Zealand

With its temperate climate and lush green countryside, New Zealand produces some of the best New World wines available on the high street today. The total production might be relatively small but it's squeaky clean and quality is dizzyingly high. What you'll find here are great sparkling wines with all the toasty complexity, elegance, and fresh fruit that's needed to rival some of the top names in Champagne.

New Zealand is split into two islands, with the North Island being the warmer of the two. From Marlborough, at the top of the South Island, come the stunningly vibrant, punchy, gooseberry-scented Sauvignon Blancs that put New Zealand firmly on the wine map a few years ago. It's also the main region for sparkling wine production. Cool nights help to keep acidity levels high, while the long, slow ripening period gives beautifully ripe but not overly fruity grapes – just the ticket for great fizz.

Some producers prefer to blend the richer wines of the North Island with the brighter, crisper wines of the South to achieve a harmonious style, taking the best from each. **The choice is yours** – The largest producer in any given country isn't usually the first port of call if you're in search of quality. So to find that Montana Wines, who produce almost half of all the wine exported from New Zealand, make some cracking fizz is further testament to the overall quality you'll find here. It's most famously sold under the "Lindauer" label, and if you want a great value alternative to Champagne, then look no further than the "Lindauer NV Special Reserve".

Other top producers to look out for

Huia Vineyards Brut

Kim Crawford Brut Rory

Miru Miru Brut
– *the name means "bubbles" in Maori.*

Pelorus
– *from the makers of the famous "Cloudy Bay" Sauvignon Blanc; this stylishly packaged sparkler rarely excites in the way you'd expect from such a producer*

Tasmania

Situated below the southeast corner of the mainland, the island of Tasmania is Australia's southernmost state and, as it's all upside-down in the Southern hemisphere, that equals the coolest. It was in the late 1980s and early 1990s that Tasmania really became known as a wine-producing region, and due to its climate and the resulting long, slow ripening period, it's sparkling wine that has emerged as the flagship style. Continued investment from Australia's big players, who have seen the potential that Tasmania has to offer in terms of sparkling wine production, looks set to guarantee a rosy future for what this state does best.

Labels to look out for

Jansz – although the range includes vintage wines, it's the NV that you're most likely to come across. Named after the skipper of Abel Tasman's flagship the Heemskerk, which in turn gave its name to the vineyard established in the Pipers River region in 1975, this wine was at one time in the hands of the Champagne house of Louis Roederer. It's a very classy fizz indeed, dominated by the Chardonnay grape and showing delicious biscuit and toast aromas along with elegant pear-style fruit. A superb alternative to Champagne.

Pirie – in stylistic contrast, Pirie is a vintage wine in which Pinot Noir plays the largest part, around seventy per cent of the blend with Chardonnay. This leads to a complex and full-bodied, green/gold wine with bold yeasty flavours and rich-apple fruit character. Again, a fizz to rival even the great Champagnes.

Tasting sparkling wine

Don't treat it in the same way as still wine. With a still wine there are three distinct steps to take to evaluate the wine.

1. Check it looks clear and bright. Swirl the wine around your glass to release the aromas and take a good long sniff.

2. Next, taste the wine, moving it all around your mouth to get the most from its flavours.

3. Spit or swallow.

With sparkling wine it's an overall impression you're after. Take a look at the bubbles, they can be delightful if they're tiny and shooting to the top of the glass. The colour may be enchanting, especially in some of the delicate rosés. Take a sip, let the wine play on your tongue, slip down your throat and create a warm sensation inside. Think about the feeling it's left you with...

A visually stunning country with some of the most beautiful and dramatic vineyard land in the world, but surely too hot for the production of decent sparkling wine? You'd think so, but it's surprising just how much South Africa's fizzy offerings have improved and started to impress over the past decade or so. In spite of the fact that it has a relatively small share of the international sparkling wine market, that share is growing rapidly and I've no doubt we'll be seeing a lot more of what the Cape has to offer on the sparkling front in the next few years.

south africa

Méthode cap classique (MCC)

Although sparkling wines are produced using all the different methods available, if you're looking for the traditional method this is its legal title in South Africa.

What you might find on the shelves

Inanda Brut – a Charmat method wine launched in 1999 with the aim of filling a perceived gap between cava and Australian sparkling wine, and intended to appeal to the cava drinker. It appears to be succeeding and currently sits in the number one spot in terms of UK sales of South African sparkling wine. Made from 100 per cent Colombard, it's a perfectly quaffable, light, and fruity, inexpensive sparkler that would no doubt go down well at any celebration.

Graham Beck Wines – established in 1983 when a South African coal magnate purchased a farm just outside Robertson in the Western Cape. The company now produces some superb MCC wines in a range that includes a NV brut and a vintage blanc de blancs. The brut is a fifty/fifty blend of Chardonnay and Pinot Noir that shows elegant, ripe-fruit flavours allied to some stylish creamy notes on the nose and palate. Fame was assured for the sparkling wines of Graham Beck when the Brut Vintage was selected for the inauguration of President Nelson Mandela in 1994.

Villiera – around twenty per cent of the production here is sparkling. The "Tradition Brut NV" is mostly Pinot Noir and has rich, smoky notes on the nose followed by a light and easygoing palate. The flagship bubbly "Monro" spends four years on its lees and is soft, creamy, and wonderfully aromatic – look out for it on your next visit to the Cape.

Twee Jonge Gezellen – winemaker Nicky Krone's own sparkling wine is the vintage-dated "Krone Borealis Brut". It is a blend of Pinot Noir and Chardonnay and as I write the 1998 is tasting deliciously forward, big, rich, and biscuity with lots of lovely bright fizz and apples-and-pears fruit.

Sparkling Sauvignon Blanc – is something you don't often see, but they make a bit of a speciality of it in South Africa. It's carbonated fizz (the bubbles will be short-lived), so forget sophistication and expect a fresh, grassy number that's a good thirst quencher on a hot afternoon

Other top prodcuers to look out for

Simonsig

Boschendal

J.C. le Roux

Steenberg

Pongrácz

Morgenhof

sparkling
etiquette

"Sparkling wine is for special occasions" – what better excuse do you need to make every day special? There's a sparkling wine out there to suit any celebration. Your budget, the time of year, who you're with, and personal preferences will all influence what to serve. On the following pages is a selection of familiar occasions with a few hints to help steer you in the right direction.

If you've ever visited Champagne, you'll know that the Champenois believe in drinking their favourite tipple from the beginning to the end of each and every meal. What a fantastic idea! At least that's what you think until three days later, when you find yourself gagging for a glass of red wine, anything, to end the barrage of acidic fizz. But Champagne and other sparkling wines are food-friendly. Here are some ideas, both classic and bizarre, for you to try.

sparkling wine with food

The link is luxury

Smoked fish – smoked salmon. One of the fuller, toastier styles of NV Champagne with a high percentage of the Pinots, perhaps even a blanc de noirs, will match well with the powerful flavours of smoked salmon.

Shellfish – oysters, scallops, crab, and lobster are all deceptively rich yet at the same time fresh, with quite a delicate taste. So let's match rather than overwhelm and choose a stylish, slightly aged blanc de blancs. Straight Chardonnay is wonderful with such luxurious shellfish.

Posh fish – turbot, halibut, John Dory. Think of weight rather than intensity of flavour and go for an elegant NV.

Caviar – if we're talking the works here, with buckwheat blinis, sour cream, grated boiled egg, candlelight, and the man (or woman) of your dreams, then rosé is the only choice. Buy vintage if you can afford it.

Canapés – the definition of a glamorous party? Endless melt-in-the-mouth canapés and a constant flow of decent Champagne.

Vintage Champagne – especially good with richer foods, having the complex biscuit and honey notes needed to stand up to strong flavours, such as guinea fowl, wild mushrooms, truffles, particularly white truffle risotto, parpadelle with a creamy rabbit sauce – oh why not?

Rosé Champagne – goes surprisingly well with sushi. If it's aged or vintage then try it with steak tartare or beef carpaccio. The *demi-sec* version makes a fabulous pudding wine for desserts that include vanilla, wild red berries, orange or shortbread.

Sparkling Shiraz – for a summer barbecue. The combination of fizz and the great outdoors is always a recipe for the immediate loss of inhibitions, so the party is guaranteed to kick off well. But the powerful smoky flavours, herby marinades, and spicy relishes are going to need the blast of fresh, black cherry fruit and edge of smoky tannin that these Aussie fizzes are full of.

Moscato d'Asti and demi-sec Champagne – both work particularly well with light, fruit-based desserts, soufflés and sorbets, the lightness of each complementing the other perfectly. The aromatic flavours of mango, passion-fruit, orange-flower water, and lychee sit well with the grapey Moscato, while a summer fruit and elderflower terrine would be delicious with the delicate sweetness of a *demi-sec*, especially served with a Champagne sabayon.

Prosecco – traditionally the Italians match this delicate, floral fizz with baked asparagus wrapped in pancetta, mild, white mountain cheeses, creamy salt cod mousse or, post dinner, with biscotti and cantuccini (biscuits). I think it works equally well as an apéritif to be sipped outdoors on a summer afternoon with a dish of toasted almonds or a plate of prosciutto.

New Zealand/Australian/Tasmanian sparklers – with the Pacific Rim flavours of lime, sweet chilli, coriander, ginger, squid, star anise, coconut, sweet potato, papaya, etc., these vibrantly fruity, New World wines, which usually exhibit the bready complexity gained from lees ageing, are definitely the answer.

Fizzy cocktails

I'm loath to suggest using Champagne in a cocktail – why spoil such a delicious drink? But if you do fancy being really decadent, then here are a few ideas to try.

Classic Champagne Cocktail

Drop a white sugar cube into the bottom of a flute glass. Soak with a few drops of Angostura bitters. Add 30ml/6 tsp of cognac and top up with chilled Champagne.

Kir Royale

Pour a small amount of crème de cassis into a flute glass, depending on how strong you like the blackcurrant flavour to be. For medium strength add no more than 1cm (⅖in) in the glass. Top up with chilled Champagne. Crème de framboise or crème de mûre work equally well.

Champagne Pick-Me-Up

Shake a shot (35ml/7 tsp) of cognac, three-quarters of a shot (25ml/5 tsp) each of freshly squeezed orange and lemon juice, and half a shot (18ml/3½ tsp) of sugar syrup with ice. Strain into a flute glass and top up with chilled Champagne. Garnish with a couple of grapes on the rim. (This recipe comes from the fantastic *Sauceguide to Cocktails* by Simon Difford.)

Classic Bellini

Put a small amount of white peach purée into a flute glass – to a depth of about 1cm (⅖in). Top up with chilled Prosecco. For a little variation choose whatever soft fruit happens to be in season, raspberry, melon, mango, or strawberry for example, to make the purée.

Scroppino

Not exactly a cocktail and used more as a palate cleanser or a dessert, in much the same way as sorbet. Simply blend lemon ice-cream, Prosecco, and a splash of vodka – delicious.

Here I'm going to be speaking predominantly to the boys. You see I'm an old-fashioned girl and I love romance the traditional way.

romantic encounters

Valentine's Day – it just has to be rosé. I know the whole thing's horribly commercial these days, but there's nothing like a glass of pink fizz to get the old juices flowing. Whether you're in a smart restaurant or the candlelight of your own kitchen, the heady mix of creamy bubbles and softly scented, red berry fruit will be irresistible, and hopefully so will you.

When proposing – this must be one of the most nerve-racking occasions, and you'll certainly need a drink post-haste, whatever the outcome. It's a once in a lifetime moment, so why not go for a *prestige cuvée* Champagne (see page 17). If your budget won't stretch – bearing in mind the forthcoming nuptials – then choose a decent NV bottle, and make sure it's in the refrigerator when you pop the question.

First date – it may seem a bit cheesy to order Champagne, but why not? (Unless you're intending to split the bill!) If she's as keen on you, as you are on her, then my guess is she'll be impressed by your style and it'll help ease those first tricky moments of conversation no end. Don't go mad, though. House Champagne will do.

Romantic dinner at home – we can become so used to the person we live with that we forget how lovely it is to be really romantic for a change. At home you can indulge in more luxurious food and wine than you might be able to afford in a restaurant, so start the evening in style and open a bottle of vintage Champagne. You might still be drinking it when you begin eating, so choose something simple, such as a lobster or crab salad.

I'm imagining relatively large occasions here, usually with a vast range of ages involved. So let's see what we can do to please everyone, while at the same time sticking to a budget.

christenings &
special birthdays

Christenings

There's inevitably a lot of expense involved with the arrival of a new baby and, of course, the possible loss of a second income if you and your partner both had jobs prior to the event. Bearing that in mind, you might just be a little bit strapped for cash by the time the christening comes around. So why not choose something a bit unusual but not too pricey? I'm sure that the grandparents, uncles, aunts, godparents, etc., will all be so taken by the sight of this tiny new member of their family, dressed up to the nines and being sprinkled with holy water, that whatever they're offered afterwards to quench their thirsts, is going to taste heavenly.

If it's an English christening, why not opt for some of the local brew and buy a case or two of English fizz to wet the baby's head? There are some stunning examples (see page 35) and the average bottle will cost about the

same as an inexpensive Champagne or a decent
bottle of sparkling New World wine. If it's a baby
girl you might even want to go for a rosé which,
as opposed to English red wine, can be a truly
delicious tipple.

How much to buy? The good news is that it's unlikely
you'll need to allow much more than half a bottle per
person given the fact that most of the older generation
tend to stick to just the odd glass, and the younger ones
will no doubt be on some brightly coloured cocktail of
non-alcoholic E numbers.

Special birthdays

The obvious answer here would be to choose a vintage
Champagne from the year of the person in question's birth.
If it's going to be a small, smart dinner party at home I'd
certainly say this is your most exciting option. For eight
to ten people, a magnum (the equivalent of two bottles)
would be terrific, sexily extravagant to the eye and large
enough to allow you a couple of generous glasses each
before dinner.

It's also worth remembering that wine in a magnum
ages more slowly than that in an ordinary bottle, which
could be an important factor in guaranteeing freshness
when we're talking about fairly old fizz.

You could always follow the theme through and
choose wines from the birth year for the entire evening
– assuming he or she is from a good vintage of course!

Whatever your budget,
a wedding is *the* occasion to
celebrate with fizz. So keep it
flowing from the beginning of the day.

weddings &
anniversaries

Weddings

Traditional – this is going to be a large event and my
advice would be to go for something relatively
inexpensive, such as Prosecco, for everyone to slurp with
their canapés. It's a lovely fizz to drink on its own or with
nibbles, having a soft apricot florality and not too much
alcohol – pretty important if you're starting early and still
intend to be around to dance the night away.

It's essential to stock up well, people will drink far
more than you'd imagine and there are plenty of places
that'll offer sale or return in case there is a whole load of
booze left at the end. Allow a bottle each of the Prosecco,
a bottle each of still wine to go with the meal and, most
importantly, at least two glasses of decent Champagne for
the toast. For the Champagne, I'd suggest trying a few
different NV brands to see which you like best. If you're
buying a large quantity then be sure to look out for
special offers a good six months before the event.

Small and select – because you'd rather keep it as intimate as possible or because you're strapped for cash and can't afford to splash out on a big do. The latter is a good excuse for a pre-wedding jaunt to Calais where you'll save a considerable amount on perfectly fine fizz.
No expense spared - I'd suggest serving a good NV Champagne from start to finish. I imagine that the food will be the focus, with a sumptuous meal following hot on the heels of luxurious canapés. You could also offer a good quality white and red still wine as an alternative.
Young and trendy – there are some funky new ways to drink Champagne, such as quarter bottles, glamorously packaged with matching straws. They are expensive, but if you have big ice-buckets full of them for people to help themselves you'll save on waiting staff costs, glass hire, washing-up and the quantity of booze, as drunk through a straw it work its magic so much faster...

Anniversaries

These become more special as the years go by, and so should the wines with which you celebrate them. The obvious thing to do is to choose a vintage Champagne from the year it all began – naturally the bigger the anniversary, the older and more exclusive the Champagne.

The great thing about fizz is that the majority of it is white. I'm convinced lots of people don't bother with a house-warming party simply because they don't want their friends to see the new pad before they've got it "just so". Once they have, of course, they're frightened to death that some over-enthusiastic guest will kick over a glass of deeply penetrating red wine. Sparkling white wine is "clearly" the answer.

house-warming &
home-coming

Three things to consider

What's your budget? It's likely to be pretty tight considering you've just spent a small fortune on moving. **What kind of food are you planning to offer?** Canapés can be an awful faff and cooking a hot meal on a new cooker for twenty-odd people, is more stress than it's worth. If you've any sense, go for a tableful of bread, cold meats, cheeses, smoked salmon and some ready-made quiches that you can stick in the oven for ten minutes. **How many people are you planning to welcome?** Invite enough people to create a good atmosphere, but not so many that your guests can't find a pew when they want to settle into a good conversation, food, and wine.

Taking these factors into consideration, if you really want fizz for your celebration, but don't want to spend more than you would on ordinary still wine, then cava is the perfect choice. Often the vintage cavas are a great deal better in terms of style and complexity than the regular NV versions, but try a few over the stressful and backbreaking course of moving home and see which you prefer. Cava is also one of those wines that's regularly on promotion, which is great when you're planning a party.

And another thing...

It's easy to remember the wine, but forget the glasses. Try ordering them from a supermarket at least a week before the party and you'll find that if you're buying the booze and food at the same time, they'll usually loan the glasses to you for free, with a deposit. Flutes are better than Paris goblets, and allow yourself enough time to pick them up and wash them. (I've never hired spotlessly clean glasses.)

Bring a bottle

If you're taking a bottle of fizz to a friend's house, make sure it's well chilled. If it's warm, one of three things can happen: 1) Your host will attempt to serve it anyway, just to be nice, and there's nothing less exciting than warm fizz. 2) It will be put in the refrigerator and served later when you've just about reached the main course stage and ought to be moving onto red. 3) It will be put in your host's wine rack for future drinking, and you miss out on it entirely.

We've already covered most of the obvious celebratory occasions that occur throughout our lives, but what about those wonderful moments that seem small but leave an everlasting memory?

celebrating
with friends

I'm thinking of events such as passing your driving test. I remember mine vividly, it was a boiling hot day and by the end of it I was literally stuck, with a combination of sweat and sheer terror, to the leatherette seat. I can't imagine a more ideal moment for a glass of chilled fizz. As it was, my mum took me for a large knickerbockerglory at the local ice-cream shop – not quite the same thing, as I'm sure you'll agree. The same could be said for passing exams or hearing that you've got your dream job: all life-changing events that we could so easily overlook celebrating.

If you decide to celebrate with a meal – either by booking a big table in a restaurant or by cooking your favourite dishes at home – then choose a wine that will complement the food. If it's Italian, how about a few good bottles of Prosecco? Spanish tapas cries out for cava. In a Thai or Chinese restaurant you need something with a bit more aroma and body, so try a good Australian, South African or New Zealand traditional method fizz.

If you're so exhausted that you simply can't face setting foot out of your own front door, I'd suggest ordering a case of Champagne to be delivered through the internet from a supermarket or high street retailer. Then, put your feet up, phone a few friends with a bring-a-bottle invitation (after all, there's never too much bubbly), and just wait for the doorbell to ring.

index